Yours Till Niagara Falls

Compiled by **LILLIAN MORRISON** • *Illustrated by* **Marjorie Bauernschmidt**

Authorized abridgement

SCHOLASTIC BOOK SERVICES

Published by Scholastic Book Services, a division
of Scholastic Magazines, Inc., New York, N.Y.

To
Aguilar
the place and the people

7th printing . . . . . . March 1966

Manufactured in the U.S.A.

Contents

PLATT

Roses are red,
Violets are blue,
Sugar is sweet,
And so are you.

Roses may be red,
Violets may be blue.
But there ain't no maybe
'Bout what I think of you.

Policeman, policeman
Do your duty!
Here comes Rosie,
The American beauty!

Fire! Fire!
False alarm.
Here comes Mazie
In a fireman's arms.

You love yourself, you think you're grand.
You go to the movies and hold your hand.
You put your arm around your waist,
And when you get fresh you slap your face.

As the years go by
And the pounds roll off,
You'll grow up to be
A real show-off.

You drink a lot of soda,
You eat a lot of cream.
But when you get older,
You'll be someone's dream.

```
2 Ys U R                                        U – R
2 Ys U B            OUQT                         2 – nice
I C U R             INVU                         2 – B
2 Ys 4 me.                                       ————————
                                                 4 – gotten
```

Blue eyes, brown hair,
Does she give the boys the air?

Marguerite, go wash your feet.
The Board of Health's across the street.

I'm not a Northern beauty,
I'm not a Southern rose.
I'm just a little schoolgirl
With freckles on my nose.

Poor little Ida
Sitting on a fence
Trying to make a dollar
Out of 99 cents.

Henry is a proper noun.
Parse it up and parse it down.
Neuter gender, hopeless case,
Object of a funny face.

Sugar is sweet,
Coal is black.
Do me a favor
And sit on a tack.

My house is situated near a pond.
Drop in some time.

Peaches grow in Florida,
California too.
But it takes a state like Iowa
To grow a peach like you.

Roses are red,
Pickles are green.
My face is a holler
But yours is a scream.

Roses are red,
Violets are blue.
When it rains
I think of you.
Drip, drip, drip.

Roses are red,
They grow in this region.
If I had your face
I'd join the Foreign Legion.

What! Write in your book!
Where gentlemen look!
Not I!
I am shy!
Goodbye!

Round went the album;
Hither it came
For me to write,
So here's my name.

Sometimes I'm naughty,
Sometimes I'm nice.
Now I'll be naughty
And sign my name thrice.

It tickles me,
It makes me laugh
To think
You want my autograph.

Lucy Brown
Lucy Brown
Lucy Brown

You asked me to sign your autograph,
But I'd rather have your photograph,
So let me know by telegraph
How you like my paragraph.

Ha! Ha! Ha! I laugh with joy,
'Cause I was here before Kilroy.

I'm the toughest boy in the city,
I'm the toughest boy in the town,
I'm the boy that spoiled your book
By writing upside down.

I bet you I can make any fool in town
Turn this album upside down.

_____
_____

Some blank verse from a blank mind.

_____

_____

_____

_____

Four lines from a lazy poet.

Alas, Alas, I am so dumb,
I cannot write in this album.

I thought, I thought, I thought in vain.
At last I thought I'd write my name.

Some write up – Some write down. But I'll be different and write around.

What! Write in your album!
What shall it be?
Just two little words
"Remember me."

(For a white page)

On this page,
Pure and white,
Only a friend would dare to write.

May you always be as pure as this page before I wrote on it.

I write on white
To be polite
And leave the yellow
For some rude fellow.

(For a blue page)

I chose BLUE
Because my friendship's true.

I hope you never feel like the color of this page.

(For a pink page)

On this page of beautiful pink
I give you a sample of Waterman's ink.

Friends, Romans, countrymen,
Lend me your ears.
Look who's graduating
After all these years.

I wasn't Bored of Education till I met you.

Open the gate!
Open the gate!
Here comes Lily
The graduate!

Birds on the mountain,
Fish in the sea.
How you ever graduated
Is a mystery to me.

When ice cream grows on spaghetti trees,
And the Sahara Desert grows muddy,
When cats and dogs wear B. V. D.'s
That's the time to study.

In days of old
When knights were bold
And teachers weren't invented,
You'd go to school
And be a fool
And come out at 3:00 contented.

Latin is a dead language.
It's plain enough to see.
It killed off all the Romans,
And now it's killing me.

Remember A,
Remember B.
Remember the day
We both got D.

Remember the fork,
Remember the spoon.
Remember the fun
In Sullivan's room.

In years to come
I'll recall memories sweet
Of the pitter patter down the hall
Of your big feet.

First we meet,
Then we part.
That's the sorrow
Of a graduate's heart

True Friends Are Like Diamonds

True friends are like diamonds,
Precious but rare;
False friends like autumn leaves
Scattered everywhere.

Tell me quick
Before I faint,
Is we friends
Or is we ain't?

Of I were a head of lettuce,
I'd cut myself in two.
I'd give the leaves to all my friends
And save the heart for you.

In the chimney of your future, please count me as a brick.

In the breadbox of your affections, regard me as a crumb.

A ring is round and has no end. So is my love for you, my friend.

There are golden ships,
There are silver ships,
But the best ship
Is "Friendship."

Love your friends, love them well,
But to your friends no secrets tell;
For if your friend becomes your foe
Your secrets everyone will know.

In the golden chain of friendship, consider me a link.

Friends are like melons.
Shall I tell you why?
To find a good one
You must one hundred try.

When you are sick
And going to die,
Call me up
And I will cry.

Until two nickels don't make a dime,
Consider yourself a friend of mine.

Not like the rose shall our friendship wither,
But like the evergreen live forever.

Remember well and bear in mind
That a faithful friend is hard to find.
And when you find one that is true
Change not the old one for the new.

I like coffee, I like tea.
I like you and you like me.

Yours till Russia cooks Turkey in Greece and
serves it on China to the Hungary U.S.A.

Yours till the bed spreads ❧ *Yours till butter flies* ❧

❧ *Yours till Bear Mountain gets cubs*

Yours till bobby pins on permanent waves get seasick

Yours till caterpillars wear roller skates ❧

❧ Yours till Cats kill Mountains

Yours till cigars box ❧ *Yours till the board walks*

Yours till Confederates wear Union suits ❧

Yours till the kitchen sinks

Yours till meatballs bounce   *Yours till the cow slips*

Yours till ginger snaps   Yours till Niagara Falls

Yours till the Statue of Liberty sits down

Yours till the United States drinks Canada Dry

Yours till the barn dances and the fire escapes

Yours till they feed the corn on your toes
to the calves of your legs

Beware of boys with eyes of brown;
They kiss you once and turn you down.
Beware of boys with eyes of blue;
They kiss you once and ask for two.
Beware of boys with eyes of gray;
They kiss you once and turn away.
Beware of boys with eyes of black;
They kiss you once and never come back.
You will know all kinds of joys
If only you'll beware of boys.

Listen, My Friend

Don't be fretful,
Don't be afraid.
Don't for my sake
Die an old maid.

Gold is pure
And so is pearl,
But purest of all
Is an innocent girl.

If you want a taste
Of heaven's joys,
Think more of the Lord
And less of the boys.

Twinkle, twinkle little star,
Eyebrow pencil, cold cream jar,
Powder puff and lipstick too
Will make a beauty out of you.

Lipstick and rouge,
Powder and paint
Make a little plain girl
Look like what she ain't.

When sitting on the sofa
With your boyfriend by your side,
Beware of false kisses,
His mustache may be dyed.

Listen my friend before we part,
Never depend on a young man's heart.
A young man's heart is like a flower,
It will wither and wilt within the hour.

There are seven ages of woman:
Diaper pins
Whip-pins
Hair pins
Fraternity pins
Diamond pins
Clothes pins
Rolling pins.
Beware of the lady of the seventh age.

There's a meter in music,
There's a meter in tone.
But the best of all meters
Is to meet 'er alone.

I love coffee
I love tea.
A shoemaker's daughter
Made a heel out of me.

Girls are like a nugget of gold,
Hard to get and hard to hold.

'Twas in a restaurant they first met,
Romeo and Juliet.
'Twas there that he got into debt
'Cause Rom-e-owed what Juli-et.

He is a fool who thinks by force or skill
To turn the current of a woman's will.

A spaniel, a woman, and a walnut tree
The more you thrash 'em, the better they be.

I love you, I love you,
I love you so well,
If I had a peanut
I'd give you the shell.

I love you, I love you,
I love you, I do.
But don't get excited,
I love monkeys too.

Pigs love pumpkins,
Cows love squash.
I love you,
I do, by gosh.

You can fall from the mountains,
You can fall from above.
But the best way to fall
Is to fall in love.

Sure as the grass grows round the stump,
You are my darling sugar lump.

My love for you
Shall never fail
As long as pussy
Has a tail.
And if that tail
Is cut in two,
That won't stop me
From loving you.

Two in a hammock
Ready to kiss,
When all of a sudden
It went like this!

Tables are round,
Chairs are square.
You and Fred Williams
Make a good pair.

I wish I were a bunny
And my tail were made of fluff.
I would jump into your vanity
And be your powder puff.

I wish I were an elephant
And you were a load of hay.
I'd put you on my great big back
And carry you away.

Your head is like a ball of straw;
Your nose is long and funny.
Your mouth is like a cellar door,
But still I love you, Honey.

If you love me as I love you,
No knife can cut our love in two.

Sitting by a stream,
Ellen had a dream.
She dreamed she was a little trout.
And some fine fellow fished her out.

I adore you.

Read	see	that	me
up	will	I	love
and	you	love	you
down	and	you	and

My ♡ pants 4 U. Of corset does.

(This is not a laundry tab
Nor marks put on teas,
But just an "I love you"
In Chinese.)

Our eyes have met,
Our lips not yet,
But oh you kid,
I'll get you yet.

Roses are red,
Violets are blue.
Lend me ten dollars,
And I will love you.

A kiss is a germ,
Or so it's been stated.
But kiss me quick,
I'm vaccinated.

When you get married
And live upstairs,
Don't come down
And borrow my chairs.

When you get married
And your husband is cross,
Pick up the broomstick
And say, "I'm the boss."

When you are married
And have a pair of twins,
Don't come to me
For safety pins.

Tom, Dick, or Harry,
Whom shall Rita marry?

Janie now, Janie ever,
Johnson now but not forever.

In after years when this you see,
I wonder what your name will be.

Gloria is your name,
Single is your station.
Happy is the lucky man
Who makes the alteration.

2 in a car,
little kisses,
weeks later,
Mr. and Mrs.

When Cupid shoots his arrow, I hope he Mrs. you.

Down by the river
Where the river flows,
There stands Alice
Pretty as a rose.
There stands Robert
By her side,
Asking her to be his bride.

If ever a husband you shall have
And he these lines should see,
Tell him of your fun in school
And kiss him twice for me.

If your husband is thirsty
And wants a drink,
Take him to the kitchen
And show him the sink.

As sure as comes your wedding day,
A broom to you I'll send.
In sunshine use the brushy part,
In storm the other end.

Needles and pins,
Triplets and twins.
When a man marries
His trouble begins.

When you are married
And have 25,
Don't call it a family,
Call it a tribe.

When you are married
And have 1, 2, 3,
Name the prettiest after me.

Sitting on a tombstone,
A ghost came and said,
"Sorry to disturb you
But you're sitting on my head."

By the sewer I lived;
By the sewer I died.
They said it was murder,
But it was sewercide.

The rooster and the chicken
Had a fight.
The chicken knocked the rooster
Out of sight.
The rooster said,
"That's all right.
I'll see you in the gumbo
Tomorrow night."

Two little boys late one night
Tried to get to Harvard on the end of a kite.
The kite string broke
And down they fell.
Instead of going to Harvard
They went to ———.
Now don't get excited
And don't get pale.
Instead of going to Harvard,
They went to Yale.

Now I lay me down to sleep
With a bag of peanuts at my feet.
If I should die before I wake
I'll leave it to my Uncle Jake.

Barbara had a cat.
It swallowed a ball of yarn.
And when the cat got kittens,
They all had sweaters on.

Ginny made some doughnuts.
She made them by the peck.
One rolled out the window
And broke the horse's neck.

Said a chambermaid to a sleeping guest
"Get up, you lazy sinner.
We need the sheet for a tablecloth
And it's almost time for dinner."

Grandma has a habit
Of chewing in her sleep.
She chews on Grandpa's whiskers
And thinks it's shredded wheat.

It's hard to lose a friend
When your heart is full of hope;
But it's worse to lose a towel
When your eyes are full of soap.

Little Kathleen took a drink,
But she shall drink no more.
For what she thought was H_2O
Was H_2SO_4!

Mary had a little car
And it was painted red.
Everywhere that Mary went
The cops picked up the dead.

Oh, I've paddled on the ocean,
I've tramped on the plain.
But I never saw a window cry
Because it had a pain.

There was a girl from Havana
Who slipped on a peel of banana.
She wanted to swear,
But her mother was there,
So she whistled "The Star Spangled Banner."

Start Low, Climb High

Start low,
Climb high.
Best of luck
In senior high.

Study and work,
Don't be a flop.
Sooner or later
You'll reach the top.

Be like a snowflake. Leave a mark but don't leave a stain.

Always be like a piano, grand, upright, and square.

Success and happiness run in pairs
If you can't find the elevator, use the stairs.

Use this ladder.

Your future lies before you
Like a shining path of snow.
Be careful how you tread
For every step will show.

If life were a thing that money could buy,
The rich would live and the poor would die.
But God in His mercy made it so
That the rich and the poor together must go.

There are three things you must learn to do:

Lie   Steal   and   Drink.

Lie in the bed of success.
Steal away from bad company.
Drink from the fountain of youth.

Be you to others kind and true
As you'd have others be to you.

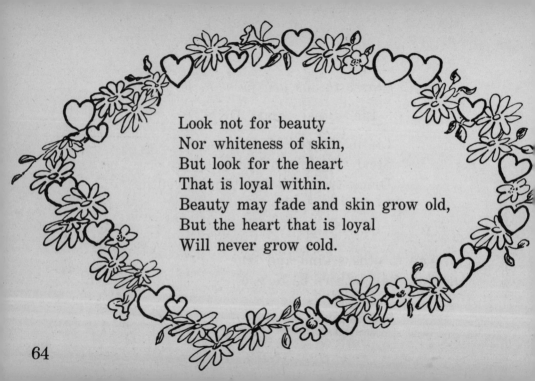

Look not for beauty
Nor whiteness of skin,
But look for the heart
That is loyal within.
Beauty may fade and skin grow old,
But the heart that is loyal
Will never grow cold.

Learn when young and not when old
For learning is better than silver and gold.
Silver and gold will vanish away
But a good education will never decay.

Don't be ⁓⁓⁓⁓⁓⁓⁓⁓ (crooked)
Don't be ✕ (cross)   Never B♯
Just be _____ (straight)   Never B♭
And you'll be boss.   Always B♮

If wisdom's ways you wisely seek,
Five things observe with care:
Of whom you speak,
To whom you speak,
And how and when and where.

Speak good English and good English will speak for you.

Love many,
Trust few.
Always paddle your own canoe.

Take the local,
Change for express.
Don't get off
Till you reach Success.

Though your tasks are many
And your rewards are few,
Remember that the mighty oak
Was once a nut like you.

Great oaks from little acorns grow
Great aches from little toe corns grow.

When times are hard,
Write me a card.
When times get better,
Write me a letter.

The past is a dream,
The present a strife;
The future a mystery,
And such is life.

Don't wait for your ship to come in. Row out and meet it.

Life is like a game of cards—

When you are in love it is ♥
When you are engaged it is ♦
When you are married it is ♣
When you are dead it is ♠

Count that day lost
Whose low descending sun
Sees from your hand
No worthy action done.

Good, better, best.
Never let it rest
Until the good is better
And the better is best.

Listen my children and you shall hear
Of the midnight ride of Sally dear.
First in a carriage, then on a wheel.
Now she rides in an automobile.

In Central Park
There is a rock,
And on it says
"Forget-me-Not."
Farther down
There is a tree,
And on it's carved,
"Remember me."

Remember me
When this you see,
And what a girl
I used to be.

Remember Grant,
Remember Lee.
The heck with them,
Remember me.

Remember me is all I ask,
But should remembrance be a task,
Forget me.

If writing in albums
Remembrance assures,
With the greatest of pleasure
I'll write in yours.

Forget the moon, forget the stars.
Forget the flirts on trolley cars.
Forget your husband's socks to mend
But don't forget your old school friend.

If you see a monkey in a tree,
Don't throw sticks, it might be me.

They say it pays to advertise.

Henry was here and is now gone,
But leaves his name to carry on.

Forget me not,
For if you do,
You'll feel the weight
Of my heavy shoe.

Remember me at the river,
Remember me at the lake.
Remember me on your wedding day,
And save me a piece of cake.

When you get old and your dress gets purple, remember the girl who wrote in a circle.

•   Dot

    Blot

Forget-me-not.

When you are in the country standing by a hedge Remember it was Trixie who wrote around the edge.

Remember the miss
Who scribbled this.

Remember the kid from Brooklyn,
Remember the kid from Spain.
Remember the kid from P.S. 10
And Judy is her name.

In your woodbox of memories, put in a chip for me.

If you have a notion
That the ocean
Is full of commotion,
Try the sea
And remember me.

As years roll by,
As years surely will,
Remember your friend
Who wrote downhill.

When you are dying
And making your will,
Think of the one
Who wrote uphill.

When you are drinking
Cold black tea,
Victoria, remember me.
And if by chance
The tea is hot,
Victoria, forget me not.

When you are washing at a tub,
Think of me with every rub.

I will not say, "Forget-me-not."
I know you will not care.
So I'll turn the saying upside down.

Forget me if you dare.

When you are old
And cannot see,
Put on your specs
And think of me.

Remember me in all your wishes,
Even when you wash the dishes.
If the water gets too hot,
Wring out the rag and forget-me-not.

Best Wishes, Amen

Can't think,
Brain dumb.
Inspiration won't come.
Poor ink,
Bum pen.
Best wishes,
Amen.

I wish you luck,
I wish you joy.
I wish you a bouncing baby boy.
And when his hair
Begins to curl,
I wish you have a baby girl.
And when her hair
Grows straight as pins,
I wish you have a pair of twins.

May your future be as bright
As Broadway at night,
And your heart be as true
As the red, white, and blue.

Best what?
I forgot.
O, of course,
Best wishes.

If you were a fish
And I were a duck,
I'd swim to the bottom
And wish you good luck.

In the storms of life
When you need an umbrella,
May you have to uphold it
A handsome young fellow.

May your luck ever spread
Like jelly on bread.

May your joys be as deep as the ocean
And your sorrows as light as its foam.
May Kansas be your dwelling place
And Heaven your future home.

May you always meet Dame Fortune,
But never her daughter Miss Fortune.

May your life be long and sunny
And your husband fat and funny.

      May your luck be like the capital of Ireland
      "Always Dublin."

May your life be a succession of successive successes.

May your life be strewn with roses
And your children have pug noses. PLATT

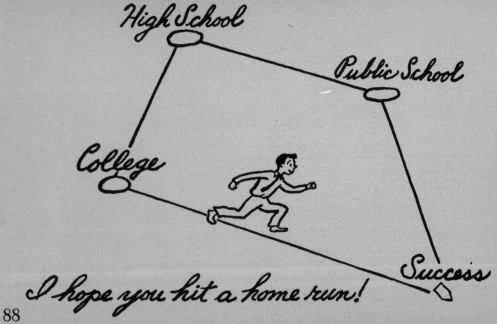

High School

Public School

College

Success

I hope you hit a home run!

Judge—Anne
Court—Public School 6
Prisoner—Connie
Cell—Room 504
Crime—Graduation
Sentence—A life of success and happiness.

Sally Smith, M.D.
Office Hours, 9 to 3

Prescription:
    Health   ⎫
    Wealth   ⎪
                 ⎬ Shake well and take in large doses.
    Happiness   ⎪
    Success   ⎭

Sailing down the stream of life
In your little bark canoe,
May you have a pleasant trip
With just room enough for two.

90

Chicken when you're hungry,
Champagne when you're dry,
A nice man when you're twenty,
And Heaven when you die.

Take the word "pluck."
Cut off the "p."
What is left
I wish for thee.

May your life be like Arithmetic:

Joys	+	(added)
Sorrows	—	(subtracted)
Happiness	X	(multiplied)
Love Un	÷	(undivided)

The Bank of Success

Pay to the order of: *Sally Jones*

The Sum of: *Health, Wealth and Happiness*

May you always be happy
And live at your ease,
And have a good husband
To tease when you please.

When the walls of earth have fallen
And this road no more we trod,
May your name in gold be written
In the autograph of God.